D1416371

ON THE MAP

WEST INDIES

Titles in This Series:

Canada	Russia
France	Spain
Italy	U.S.A.
Japan	West Indies

Editor: Frank Tarsitano
Design: M&M Partnership
Photographs: Zefa except: Allsport (25tr, 29tr),
Chris Fairclough (111, 19tl), Robert Harding (17t,
23t), Image Bank (11r), Spectrum (26br)
Map artwork: Raymond Turvey
Cover photo: *Martinique*

Library of Congress Cataloging-in-Publication Data

Flint, David, l946-
    West Indies / written by David Flint.
      p. cm. — (On the map)
    Includes index.
    Summary: Presents an overview of the geography, weather,
people, and culture of the West Indies.
      ISBN 0–8114–2942–3
      1. West Indies — Juvenile literature.   [1. West Indies.]
    I. Title.   II. Series.
    F1608.3.F58   1993
    917.29–dc20   92-43914
                                                   CIP   AC

Typeset by Multifacit Graphics, Keyport, NJ
Printed and bound in the United States
1 2 3 4 5 6 7 8 9 0 VH 98 97 96 95 94 93

WEST INDIES

David Flint

RSVP
**RAINTREE
STECK-VAUGHN**
P U B L I S H E R S
The Steck-Vaughn Company
Austin, Texas

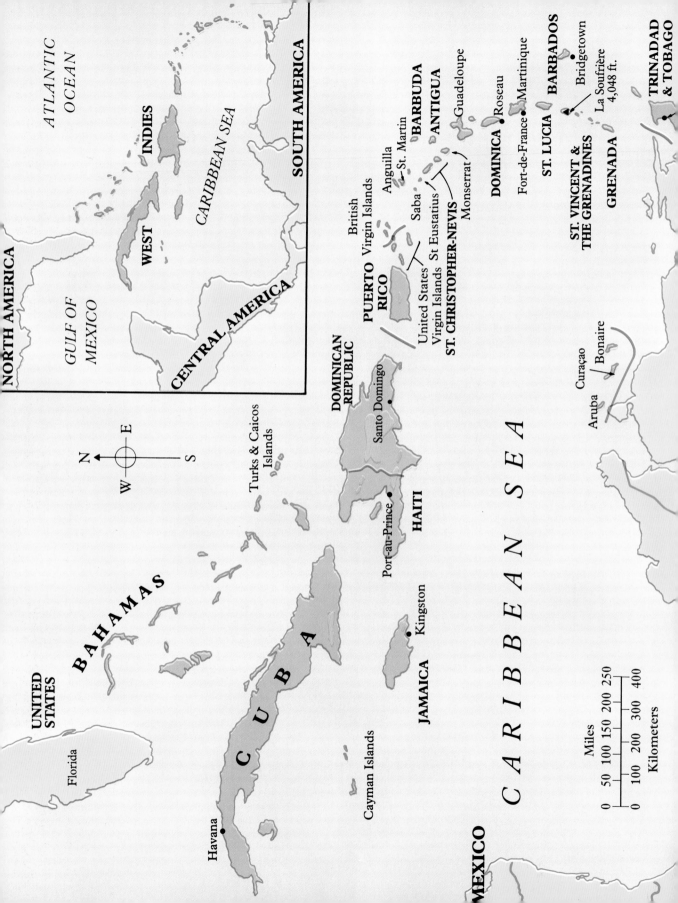

ATLANTIC
OCEAN

WEST INDIES

CARIBBEAN SEA

NORTH AMERICA

SOUTH AMERICA

CENTRAL AMERICA

GULF OF
MEXICO

N
W ⊕ E
S

UNITED
STATES

Florida

Havana

C U B A

BAHAMAS

Cayman Islands

JAMAICA   Kingston

Turks & Caicos
Islands

HAITI

Port-au-Prince

DOMINICAN
REPUBLIC

Santo Domingo

PUERTO
RICO

British
Virgin Islands

United States
Virgin Islands
ST. CHRISTOPHER-NEVIS

Anguilla
St. Martin

Saba
St Eustatius
Monserrat

BARBUDA
ANTIGUA

Guadeloupe

DOMINICA   Roseau

Fort-de-France   Martinique

ST. LUCIA   BARBADOS

Bridgetown

La Soufrière
4,048 ft.

ST. VINCENT &
THE GRENADINES

GRENADA

Aruba

Curaçao
Bonaire

TRINIDAD
& TOBAGO

C A R I B B E A N   S E A

MEXICO

Miles
0 50 100 150 200 250
0 100 200 300 400
Kilometers

Contents

Island Countries

There are thousands of islands stretched out across the Caribbean Sea between North and South America. These are the islands of the West Indies, which are home to 35 million people.

The islands are very different. Some are flat while others are mountainous. Some are covered with thick, steamy rain forests, and others are as dry as a desert. Many of the islands in the West Indies are actually the tops of an undersea chain of mountains. They stretch from North to South America.

Cuba is the largest island, but others are so tiny they do not appear on many maps. The larger islands, like Cuba, Hispaniola, Jamaica, and Puerto Rico, have millions of people. The smallest of islands may not have people living on them at all.

To the north of the Caribbean is the United States, with Florida the closest state of all. To the west is Mexico and Central America, and then to the south are countries like Venezuela and Colombia in South America. To the east lies the Atlantic Ocean.

The big islands have large cities and seaports. The smaller islands have smaller towns and cities, but some islands have no towns at all.

St. Lucia is a favorite stop for cruise ships in the West Indies.
Trips to nearby mountains or bays are always popular.

Grenada and St. Vincent are covered
with tall palm trees. Small bays and
harbors dot the coasts of these
islands.

No two islands are the same. Some
like Beef Island and Guana Island,
shown here, are small.

Diamond Strand Beach in Martinique is famous for its sandy beaches, palm trees, and blue sky.

These sharp jagged peaks of ancient volcanoes have been covered by forests on St. Lucia.

Many islands are the tops of volcanoes like this one on the island of St. Vincent.

Mountains, Volcanoes, and Beaches

High mountains with steep sides are found on many of the islands. The highest mountain in the area is on the island of Hispaniola. This mountain is called Duarte Peak and it is 10,414 feet high. Around the coasts, there are lots of bays with bright, sandy beaches. The sunshine, together with the beaches, the warm seas, and the spectacular scenery attracts many tourists each year.

On the island of St. Vincent, there is a volcano called La Soufrière. You can smell sulfur in the steam and smoke that rise from the crater at the top of the volcano. The word "soufrière" means "sulfur mine" in French. La Soufrière is an active volcano. Most of these volcanoes are not active. That means they have not erupted for years and may never erupt again.

Fine bays, inlets, and harbors cut into the coastlines of many of these islands, giving ships and boats good places to anchor. Long stretches of bright sandy beaches line the shores along the clear blue waters of the Caribbean Sea. Thousands of visitors from all over the world flock to these beaches throughout the year to swim, fish, and sunbathe. Taking care of these visitors is a very important business in the West Indies.

The Weather

The weather is hot for most of the year in the West Indies, with temperatures of 75°F or more. Nights are cooler, but most people wear thin clothes all the time. The dry season is from January to June. Then, cracks open up in the baked ground and tar on streets melts in the fierce heat.

Some islands in the West Indies get rain every day of the year. Other islands get very little rain at all. The size, shape, and location of an island help determine how much rain it gets. Many islands have dry and rainy seasons. The average rainfall throughout the region is about 60 inches a year. But some places get more than 200 inches a year.

Hurricanes are one of the biggest dangers. Strong forces build up in towering black clouds bringing fierce winds and torrential rain. The strengthening winds uproot trees, overturn cars, and demolish buildings. Suddenly, all goes quiet and the wind drops. This is the eye of the hurricane—but wait! As the storm moves on, the tempest begins again.

The hurricane season begins in late summer and can last into November. Weather forecasters try to predict when storms are coming so people can be prepared.

People board up windows when a hurricane is forecast, even though the sun is still shining.

When the storm has passed, it is time to repair the walls, windows, and roofs.

A hurricane batters the coast as it whips up the ocean.

Peoples

The first people to live on the islands were the Arawaks and the Caribs. The Arawaks were a peaceful people who came to the islands from Central and South America. The Caribs reached the islands 1,000 years after the Arawaks. When Columbus landed in 1492, the tribes had been living there for over 1,800 years.

Columbus did not know he had landed in a new world. He called the Native Americans he met Indians because he thought he had landed in the Indies, islands off the coast of Asia. These islands are called the West Indies, while the islands off the coast of Asia are called the East Indies.

Spanish invaders followed, looking for gold. They forced the islanders to work as slaves on farms and in mines. Many died from overwork and new diseases brought by the Europeans. Later French, English, and Dutch invaders arrived. They drove the tribes off the land and built farms and houses. Soon they brought slaves from Africa to work on the European farms.

Now descendants of the Africans form the largest group on the islands. Other groups include descendants of Indian and Chinese workers and descendants of Europeans. Only a few Caribs and Arawaks remain.

The great grandparents of these banana sellers came from Africa as slaves.

The West Indies has people from many ethnic origins. This girl is at a carnival in Port-au-Prince, Haiti.

This mailbox in Curaçao is a reminder of the island's Dutch heritage.

Sugarcane was first grown on farms worked by slaves. Today, the cane is still harvested by hand on Haiti.

Coffee from the Blue Mountains of Jamaica is prized all over the world. The coffee beans are picked as soon as they are ripe.

Fishing is very important in the West Indies. The fish are sold fresh from their boats.

Cacao pods ripen on a tree in Jamaica. Cacao is used to make cocoa and chocolate.

Farming and Fishing

Farming is vital to all the islands, and many people grow their own food. Yams, sweet potatoes, tomatoes, and plantains are grown for the family or for sale at the local market. Other crops, like bananas and cocoa, are grown for sale abroad.

Bananas are picked when they are hard and green. Refrigerated ships then carry the fruits to America or Europe where they ripen in special warehouses. Trucks take them to supermarkets and fruit markets—where we can buy them.

Sugar, coffee, and tobacco are important crops on the islands. These crops are usually grown on large farms often called plantations. Many people work on a large plantation, and most of the crop is exported to other countries. Sugar is the most important export crop in the islands. Sugar sales bring millions of dollars into the islands every year.

Fish are caught around all the islands and are sold fresh, or preserved in salt. Lobster is a delicacy in St. Lucia. Every day fishing boats sail out to harvest tuna, bonito, lobster, and crabs. Although some fish is eaten by the islanders, most is sold to other countries.

Natural Riches

The two best natural resources of the West Indies are the climate and the land. The climate, with its warm temperatures, attracts tourists. The rich land and good rainfall is perfect for farming. But these islands have some other natural resources, too.

The islands also have many valuable minerals. Oil from wells around Trinidad is refined on the island and has helped make it rich. The industry offers good jobs which attract people from the farms to towns like Port of Spain. Now Trinidad buys more food from other countries instead of growing its own.

Trinidad also has the world's largest asphalt lake. It is called Pitch Lake. Asphalt is a thick oil-like substance used to surface roads in the United States and Europe.

Jamaicans mine a mineral called bauxite. They are the third largest producer in the world. Bauxite is a reddish mineral used to make aluminum. Aluminum is used in everything from pots and pans to airplanes. Therefore, bauxite is a very valuable resource. Most Jamaican bauxite is shipped to other countries. The sale of this resource brings money into Jamaica, so Jamaicans often called bauxite "red gold."

Trinidad has the world's largest asphalt lake, called Pitch Lake.

Oil from island wells goes
to refineries like this one
on the Virgin Islands.

Bauxite mining is a very important
industry in Jamaica.

On the Move

Cities on richer islands like Puerto Rico or Trinidad are often crowded with traffic. These islands have more cars, cheap gasoline, and good roads.

On other islands and in the countryside where most people are farmers, it is quieter. There are few cars, and people walk, or ride horses or donkeys. Horses and donkeys are used to pull heavy loads. Buses link villages with towns and cities.

There are many good harbors in the West Indies, and traveling by boat is common. Large tourist ships slide through Caribbean waters bringing thousands of tourists to the islands. These ships dock at lively and inviting ports while visitors go ashore to see the sights and spend money.

People use boats like a bus service beween islands. The boats are big enough to carry crops to markets in cities and towns. Since the islands are spread out over 2,000 miles, going from place to place by airplane is common. All the major cities have airports large enough to handle big jet planes. Many islands have smaller landing fields for smaller planes. These "puddle-jumpers" fly from island to island taking tourists almost anywhere they want to go.

Water travel between islands is very important. Ferries like this one link small islands with the main ones.

In many places, people have to walk long distances to work, to school, or to the markets.

The airport at St. Thomas on the Virgin Islands—small planes have become a vital link between the thousands of islands.

Modern towns have many different types of traffic, from cars and buses to motorcycles and even boats.

Tourist resorts like St. Croix on the Virgin Islands provide jobs for local people in hotels and restaurants.

People who work on the land sell their goods in markets like this one on Grenada.

Some people have skilled jobs in modern industries like this oil refinery on Curaçao.

Sugarcane is unloaded at the processing factory on Barbados. The sugar is sold worldwide.

Work

In the West Indies, three out of every five workers work on the land. Others work in a factory or office, or in a shop or hotel. Some people own their own land, but often their farms are small. A few huge farms, called plantations, grow bananas, sugarcane, tobacco, or coffee. These are owned by rich people or often by large foreign companies.

Many people have jobs in the tourist industry. These people work in hotels, restaurants, and stores—taking care of the more than eight million people who visit the islands every year. Workers can also find jobs at airports and seaports where there are tourists.

On islands like Barbados and Puerto Rico, people work in factories which make clothes, plastics, and machines. On Trinidad, cars are assembled from kits that come from Japan. Some island people work in mines and others work in the oil fields. All over the islands many people work in hotels and restaurants.

On the whole, these islands are not known for their manufactured products. Most islands are too small to have factories and large businesses. Thus many manufactured goods are imported from other countries.

Going to School

Education is important to all the countries of the West Indies. Parents hope their children will work hard and find a good job. Most schools are in the towns, so buses take children from remote villages to their schools. However, some children still have an hour's walk just to reach school.

On most islands education is free. Students on some islands attend school in shifts, so that all get into school.

Schoolchildren sometimes teach reading and writing to older people who have never had the chance to go to school. In countries like Cuba, many schools have farms which are run by the pupils. Other schools teach students a skill or a trade, such as how to be an auto mechanic.

Most children speak at least two languages. In countries that were once French-speaking, like Haiti, or that still belong to France, classes are taught in French. On other islands classes are taught in Spanish or English. Sometimes students speak a completely different language at home and then English, Spanish, or French in school.

These friends take a break from lessons in a Jamaican elementary school.

Most schools have a uniform like this one in St. Lucia.

Leisure Time

With so many beautiful beaches and such good weather, the islanders are experts at water sports. These sports include diving, windsurfing, or snorkeling. But people of the West Indies enjoy life in many other ways, like hiking, or camping, or inviting friends for dinner. Even board games like checkers and chess are popular.

Baseball is one of the most popular sports in the islands. It is especially popular in Cuba, in Puerto Rico, and in the Dominican Republic. Many major league players in the United States got their start by playing baseball in the West Indies.

Soccer is played on most of the islands. In many places soccer is a more popular sport than baseball. Soccer is played in schools and colleges. There are also professional soccer teams in the West Indies. Sometimes teams from one country play teams from another country.

Cricket is played on those islands where the English once ruled or still rule. Cricket is a very English game. There are eleven players on a cricket team, and there is a ball and bat. But the game is nothing like our game of baseball.

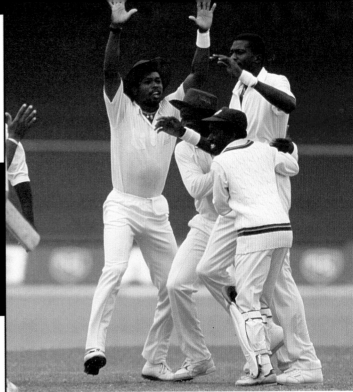

People of the West Indies enjoy their beautiful sandy beaches and warm blue water.

The West Indies cricket team celebrates after a winning game.

A cooling swim at the Dunn's River Falls on Jamaica.

On some islands, like Jamaica, water sports are enjoyed by local people.

A colorful parade in Fort-de-France on the island of Martinique.

Many hours are spent preparing for the carnival in Trinidad.

Everyone takes part in the carnival with dances, music, and fun.

A steel band in Bridgetown, Barbados. The instruments are made from old oil drums.

Carnival and Calypso

People of the West Indies love to celebrate with friends, visitors, or strangers. The Trinidad carnival is one of the biggest celebrations in the islands—and one of the most magnificent spectacles in the world. It happens each year just before Lent. Thousands of people flood the streets singing, dancing, and having fun. All kinds of good foods are cooked and sold. People of all ages dress up in fancy costumes, and parades last all day.

There are parades, with stunning costumes, dancing to the music of steel bands, and calypso—amusing folk songs about local events. Calypso is a special kind of music that is a mixture of African, Spanish, and American music.

Not all the islands celebrate at the same time or even in the same way. Martinique's carnival begins on Ash Wednesday, when people dress as black and white devils. In the Bahamas and Jamaica parades for Junkanoo, an Arawak god, are held near Christmas.

A carnival celebration on some islands in the West Indies can last two or three days, like the Mardi Gras celebration in New Orleans.

Famous Landmarks

This monument honors Haiti's slaves who revolted against French rule.

These homes in Guamo on Cuba show how the Arawak and Caribs lived long ago.

The West Indies cricket team in Barbados. Cricket is a very popular sport on some islands.

Martinique is part of France and sends representatives to the French government in Paris.

Devon House, a 19th century colonial mansion in Kingston, Jamaica.

These modern apartments are in Havana, Cuba. Over 2 million people live in the island's capital.

Facts and Figures

The West Indies—the Land and People

Population:	35 million
Largest Island:	Cuba—44,218 square miles
Languages:	Spanish, French, English, Dutch, Creole, and local dialects such as Papiamento (a mixture of different Creole languages and Spanish)
Religions:	Protestant, Catholic, Hindu, Rastafarian, and others.

Countries of the West Indies

Country	Capital City (official language)
Antigua & Barbuda	St. John's (English)
Bahamas	Nassau (English)
Barbados	Bridgetown (English)
Cuba	Havana (Spanish)
Dominica	Roseau (English, Creole)
Dominican Republic	Santo Domingo (Spanish)
Grenada	St. George's (English)
Haiti	Port-au-Prince (French)
Jamaica	Kingston (English)
St. Christopher-Nevis	Basseterre (English)
St. Lucia	Castries (English)
St. Vincent & the Grenadines	Kingstown (English)
Trinidad & Tobago	Port of Spain (English)

What Happened When

Date	Event
500 B.C.	Early Arawak settlers arrive
1300 A.D.	Caribs settle on some islands
1492	Columbus lands on the Bahamas
1494	Spanish, English, French, and Dutch settle on the West Indies. They drive out or kill off the surviving Caribs and Arawaks and import slaves from Africa to work on the plantation.
1804	Slaves in Haiti revolt against French and set up an independent country. Gradually slavery is abolished throughout the region.
1865	Dominican Republic becomes an independent country followed slowly by other islands in the West Indies.

Some remain dependent territories:
Great Britain—Anguilla, Bermuda, the British Virgin Islands, the Cayman Islands, Monserrat, Turks, and Caicos Islands.
The Netherlands—Aruba, Bonaire, Curaçao, Saba, St. Eustatius, and the southern part of St. Martin.
United States—the United States Virgin Islands. Puerto Rico is a self-governing commonwealth in union with the United States.

The following are overseas departments of **France**: Guadeloupe, Martinique, and the northern part of St. Martin.

Average Temperatures in Fahrenheit

City and Country	January	June
Roseau, Dominica	64°F	86°F
Havana, Cuba	50°F	80°F
Kingston, Jamaica	59°F	84°F
Port of Spain, Trinidad, and Tobago	72°F	80°F

Further Reading

Books

Antigua and Barbuda. Chelsea House, 1988

Broberg, Merle. *Barbados.* Chelsea House, 1989

Brothers, Don. *West Indies.* Chelsea House, 1989

Haverstock, Nathan A. *The Dominican Republic in Pictures.* Lerner, 1988

Law, Kevin. *St. Lucia.* Chelsea, 1988

Lye, Keith. *Take a Trip to the West Indies.* Watts, 1984

Index